50 Homemade Pizza Recipes for All Tastes

By: Kelly Johnson

Table of Contents

- Margherita Pizza
- Pepperoni Pizza
- BBQ Chicken Pizza
- Veggie Supreme Pizza
- Hawaiian Pizza
- Mushroom and Spinach Pizza
- Meat Lovers Pizza
- White Garlic Pizza
- Buffalo Chicken Pizza
- Pesto Chicken Pizza
- Four Cheese Pizza
- Mediterranean Pizza
- Sausage and Peppers Pizza
- Caprese Pizza
- Shrimp Scampi Pizza
- Margherita with Arugula Pizza
- Chicken Alfredo Pizza
- Italian Sausage Pizza
- Spinach and Ricotta Pizza
- Taco Pizza
- Fajita Chicken Pizza
- Prosciutto and Arugula Pizza
- Smoked Salmon Pizza
- Eggplant Parmesan Pizza
- BBQ Beef Pizza
- Bacon and Onion Pizza
- Roasted Garlic and Rosemary Pizza
- Veggie Pesto Pizza
- Peppadew and Goat Cheese Pizza
- Breakfast Pizza
- Zaa'tar Pizza
- Ranch Chicken Pizza
- Cheeseburger Pizza
- Sweet Potato and Bacon Pizza
- Buffalo Cauliflower Pizza

- Greek Pizza
- Fig and Prosciutto Pizza
- Caramelized Onion and Blue Cheese Pizza
- Spicy Sausage Pizza
- Pear and Gorgonzola Pizza
- Chicken Caesar Pizza
- Hot Honey and Pepperoni Pizza
- Vegan Margherita Pizza
- Ricotta and Lemon Zest Pizza
- Lobster and Lemon Pizza
- Chili and Cheese Pizza
- Puttanesca Pizza
- Roasted Beet and Goat Cheese Pizza
- Cilantro Lime Chicken Pizza
- Balsamic Glazed Chicken Pizza

Margherita Pizza

Ingredients:

- 1 pizza dough (store-bought or homemade)
- 1/2 cup pizza sauce
- 1 1/2 cups fresh mozzarella cheese, sliced
- Fresh basil leaves
- Olive oil, for drizzling
- Salt and pepper, to taste

Instructions:

1. Preheat oven to 475°F (245°C).
2. Roll out the pizza dough on a floured surface to your desired thickness.
3. Place the dough on a pizza stone or baking sheet.
4. Spread pizza sauce evenly over the dough.
5. Arrange the mozzarella slices on top of the sauce.
6. Bake for 10-12 minutes until the crust is golden and the cheese is melted.
7. Remove from the oven and top with fresh basil leaves. Drizzle with olive oil and season with salt and pepper.
8. Slice and serve.

Pepperoni Pizza

Ingredients:

- 1 pizza dough
- 1/2 cup pizza sauce
- 2 cups shredded mozzarella cheese
- 1/2 cup sliced pepperoni
- Olive oil, for drizzling

Instructions:

1. Preheat oven to 475°F (245°C).
2. Roll out the pizza dough on a floured surface and transfer to a pizza stone or baking sheet.
3. Spread pizza sauce evenly over the dough.
4. Sprinkle mozzarella cheese on top of the sauce.
5. Arrange pepperoni slices over the cheese.
6. Bake for 10-12 minutes until the crust is golden and the cheese is bubbly.
7. Remove from the oven, drizzle with olive oil, slice, and serve.

BBQ Chicken Pizza

Ingredients:

- 1 pizza dough
- 1/2 cup BBQ sauce
- 2 cups cooked, shredded chicken
- 1/2 red onion, thinly sliced
- 1 1/2 cups shredded mozzarella cheese
- 1/2 cup sliced cilantro

Instructions:

1. Preheat oven to 475°F (245°C).
2. Roll out the pizza dough and place it on a pizza stone or baking sheet.
3. Spread BBQ sauce evenly over the dough.
4. Top with shredded chicken, red onion slices, and mozzarella cheese.
5. Bake for 10-12 minutes until the crust is golden and the cheese is melted.
6. Remove from the oven and top with fresh cilantro. Slice and serve.

Veggie Supreme Pizza

Ingredients:

- 1 pizza dough
- 1/2 cup pizza sauce
- 1 1/2 cups shredded mozzarella cheese
- 1/4 cup bell peppers, diced
- 1/4 cup red onion, thinly sliced
- 1/4 cup mushrooms, sliced
- 1/4 cup black olives, sliced
- Fresh spinach leaves
- Olive oil, for drizzling

Instructions:

1. Preheat oven to 475°F (245°C).
2. Roll out the pizza dough on a floured surface and transfer to a pizza stone or baking sheet.
3. Spread pizza sauce over the dough and sprinkle with mozzarella cheese.
4. Arrange bell peppers, red onion, mushrooms, black olives, and spinach over the cheese.
5. Bake for 10-12 minutes until the crust is golden and the cheese is melted.
6. Drizzle with olive oil and serve.

Hawaiian Pizza

Ingredients:

- 1 pizza dough
- 1/2 cup pizza sauce
- 1 1/2 cups shredded mozzarella cheese
- 1 cup cooked ham, diced
- 1/2 cup pineapple chunks (drained)
- Olive oil, for drizzling

Instructions:

1. Preheat oven to 475°F (245°C).
2. Roll out the pizza dough and place on a pizza stone or baking sheet.
3. Spread pizza sauce over the dough and sprinkle with mozzarella cheese.
4. Add diced ham and pineapple chunks over the cheese.
5. Bake for 10-12 minutes until the crust is golden and the cheese is bubbly.
6. Drizzle with olive oil, slice, and serve.

Mushroom and Spinach Pizza

Ingredients:

- 1 pizza dough
- 1/2 cup pizza sauce
- 1 1/2 cups shredded mozzarella cheese
- 1 cup mushrooms, sliced
- 1 cup fresh spinach leaves
- Olive oil, for drizzling

Instructions:

1. Preheat oven to 475°F (245°C).
2. Roll out the pizza dough and transfer to a pizza stone or baking sheet.
3. Spread pizza sauce evenly over the dough.
4. Sprinkle mozzarella cheese on top, then layer with sliced mushrooms and spinach leaves.
5. Bake for 10-12 minutes until the crust is golden and the cheese is melted.
6. Drizzle with olive oil and serve.

Meat Lovers Pizza

Ingredients:

- 1 pizza dough
- 1/2 cup pizza sauce
- 2 cups shredded mozzarella cheese
- 1/4 cup cooked sausage, crumbled
- 1/4 cup pepperoni slices
- 1/4 cup cooked bacon, crumbled
- 1/4 cup cooked ham, diced

Instructions:

1. Preheat oven to 475°F (245°C).
2. Roll out the pizza dough and place on a pizza stone or baking sheet.
3. Spread pizza sauce evenly over the dough and top with shredded mozzarella cheese.
4. Add sausage, pepperoni, bacon, and ham over the cheese.
5. Bake for 10-12 minutes until the crust is golden and the cheese is bubbly.
6. Slice and serve.

White Garlic Pizza

Ingredients:

- 1 pizza dough
- 1/2 cup olive oil
- 3 cloves garlic, minced
- 1 1/2 cups ricotta cheese
- 1 cup shredded mozzarella cheese
- Fresh basil, for garnish

Instructions:

1. Preheat oven to 475°F (245°C).
2. Roll out the pizza dough and transfer it to a pizza stone or baking sheet.
3. Heat olive oil in a small pan and sauté garlic until fragrant. Brush the garlic oil over the pizza dough.
4. Spread ricotta cheese over the dough, followed by mozzarella cheese.
5. Bake for 10-12 minutes until the crust is golden and the cheese is melted.
6. Garnish with fresh basil, slice, and serve.

Buffalo Chicken Pizza

Ingredients:

- 1 pizza dough
- 1/2 cup buffalo sauce
- 2 cups cooked, shredded chicken
- 1 1/2 cups shredded mozzarella cheese
- 1/4 red onion, thinly sliced
- Blue cheese crumbles, for garnish

Instructions:

1. Preheat oven to 475°F (245°C).
2. Roll out the pizza dough and place it on a pizza stone or baking sheet.
3. Toss shredded chicken in buffalo sauce and spread it over the dough.
4. Sprinkle mozzarella cheese on top, then add sliced red onion.
5. Bake for 10-12 minutes until the crust is golden and the cheese is melted.
6. Garnish with blue cheese crumbles, slice, and serve.

Pesto Chicken Pizza

Ingredients:

- 1 pizza dough
- 1/2 cup pesto sauce
- 1 1/2 cups shredded mozzarella cheese
- 1 cup cooked chicken, sliced
- 1/4 cup sun-dried tomatoes, chopped
- Fresh basil leaves, for garnish

Instructions:

1. Preheat oven to 475°F (245°C).
2. Roll out the pizza dough and place it on a pizza stone or baking sheet.
3. Spread pesto sauce evenly over the dough.
4. Top with shredded mozzarella cheese, sliced chicken, and sun-dried tomatoes.
5. Bake for 10-12 minutes until the crust is golden and the cheese is melted.
6. Garnish with fresh basil leaves, slice, and serve.

Four Cheese Pizza

Ingredients:

- 1 pizza dough
- 1/2 cup pizza sauce
- 1/2 cup shredded mozzarella cheese
- 1/2 cup shredded cheddar cheese
- 1/2 cup grated Parmesan cheese
- 1/2 cup ricotta cheese
- Olive oil, for drizzling

Instructions:

1. Preheat oven to 475°F (245°C).
2. Roll out the pizza dough and transfer to a pizza stone or baking sheet.
3. Spread pizza sauce over the dough and sprinkle with mozzarella, cheddar, Parmesan, and ricotta cheeses.
4. Drizzle with olive oil.
5. Bake for 10-12 minutes until the crust is golden and the cheese is bubbly.
6. Slice and serve.

Mediterranean Pizza

Ingredients:

- 1 pizza dough
- 1/2 cup hummus
- 1 1/2 cups shredded mozzarella cheese
- 1/4 cup kalamata olives, pitted and sliced
- 1/4 cup sun-dried tomatoes, chopped
- 1/4 cup red onion, thinly sliced
- Fresh spinach leaves
- Olive oil, for drizzling

Instructions:

1. Preheat oven to 475°F (245°C).
2. Roll out the pizza dough and place it on a pizza stone or baking sheet.
3. Spread hummus over the dough.
4. Top with shredded mozzarella cheese, olives, sun-dried tomatoes, red onion, and spinach.
5. Bake for 10-12 minutes until the crust is golden and the cheese is melted.
6. Drizzle with olive oil, slice, and serve.

Sausage and Peppers Pizza

Ingredients:

- 1 pizza dough
- 1/2 cup pizza sauce
- 2 cups shredded mozzarella cheese
- 1/2 cup cooked sausage, crumbled
- 1/4 cup red bell pepper, sliced
- 1/4 cup green bell pepper, sliced
- 1/4 cup red onion, thinly sliced
- Olive oil, for drizzling

Instructions:

1. Preheat oven to 475°F (245°C).
2. Roll out the pizza dough and transfer to a pizza stone or baking sheet.
3. Spread pizza sauce over the dough and sprinkle with mozzarella cheese.
4. Add crumbled sausage, bell peppers, and red onion over the cheese.
5. Bake for 10-12 minutes until the crust is golden and the cheese is bubbly.
6. Drizzle with olive oil, slice, and serve.

Caprese Pizza

Ingredients:

- 1 pizza dough
- 1/2 cup pizza sauce
- 1 1/2 cups fresh mozzarella cheese, sliced
- Fresh tomatoes, sliced
- Fresh basil leaves
- Olive oil, for drizzling
- Balsamic glaze, for drizzling

Instructions:

1. Preheat oven to 475°F (245°C).
2. Roll out the pizza dough and place it on a pizza stone or baking sheet.
3. Spread pizza sauce over the dough.
4. Top with mozzarella slices and arrange fresh tomato slices on top.
5. Bake for 10-12 minutes until the crust is golden and the cheese is melted.
6. Garnish with fresh basil leaves, drizzle with olive oil and balsamic glaze, slice, and serve.

Shrimp Scampi Pizza

Ingredients:

- 1 pizza dough
- 1/2 cup Alfredo sauce
- 2 cups shredded mozzarella cheese
- 1 cup cooked shrimp, peeled and deveined
- 2 cloves garlic, minced
- 1/4 cup fresh parsley, chopped
- Lemon zest, for garnish

Instructions:

1. Preheat oven to 475°F (245°C).
2. Roll out the pizza dough and transfer to a pizza stone or baking sheet.
3. Spread Alfredo sauce evenly over the dough.
4. Top with mozzarella cheese, cooked shrimp, minced garlic, and parsley.
5. Bake for 10-12 minutes until the crust is golden and the cheese is melted.
6. Garnish with lemon zest, slice, and serve.

Margherita with Arugula Pizza

Ingredients:

- 1 pizza dough
- 1/2 cup pizza sauce
- 1 1/2 cups fresh mozzarella cheese, sliced
- Fresh basil leaves
- Fresh arugula, for garnish
- Olive oil, for drizzling
- Salt and pepper, to taste

Instructions:

1. Preheat oven to 475°F (245°C).
2. Roll out the pizza dough and place on a pizza stone or baking sheet.
3. Spread pizza sauce over the dough.
4. Arrange mozzarella slices on top.
5. Bake for 10-12 minutes until the crust is golden and the cheese is melted.
6. After baking, top with fresh arugula, basil leaves, and a drizzle of olive oil. Season with salt and pepper.
7. Slice and serve.

Chicken Alfredo Pizza

Ingredients:

- 1 pizza dough
- 1/2 cup Alfredo sauce
- 2 cups shredded mozzarella cheese
- 1 cup cooked chicken, sliced
- 1/4 cup spinach, sautéed
- Olive oil, for drizzling

Instructions:

1. Preheat oven to 475°F (245°C).
2. Roll out the pizza dough and transfer to a pizza stone or baking sheet.
3. Spread Alfredo sauce evenly over the dough.
4. Sprinkle mozzarella cheese on top, then add cooked chicken and sautéed spinach.
5. Bake for 10-12 minutes until the crust is golden and the cheese is melted.
6. Drizzle with olive oil, slice, and serve.

Italian Sausage Pizza

Ingredients:

- 1 pizza dough
- 1/2 cup pizza sauce
- 2 cups shredded mozzarella cheese
- 1/2 cup Italian sausage, crumbled
- 1/4 cup red onion, thinly sliced
- 1/4 cup green bell pepper, sliced
- Red pepper flakes, for garnish

Instructions:

1. Preheat oven to 475°F (245°C).
2. Roll out the pizza dough and place it on a pizza stone or baking sheet.
3. Spread pizza sauce over the dough.
4. Sprinkle mozzarella cheese, crumbled sausage, onion, and bell pepper on top.
5. Bake for 10-12 minutes until the crust is golden and the cheese is melted.
6. Garnish with red pepper flakes, slice, and serve.

Spinach and Ricotta Pizza

Ingredients:

- 1 pizza dough
- 1/2 cup pizza sauce
- 1 1/2 cups ricotta cheese
- 1 1/2 cups shredded mozzarella cheese
- 1 cup fresh spinach, sautéed
- Olive oil, for drizzling

Instructions:

1. Preheat oven to 475°F (245°C).
2. Roll out the pizza dough and place it on a pizza stone or baking sheet.
3. Spread pizza sauce over the dough.
4. Top with ricotta and mozzarella cheeses.
5. Add sautéed spinach on top of the cheese.
6. Bake for 10-12 minutes until the crust is golden and the cheese is melted.
7. Drizzle with olive oil, slice, and serve.

Taco Pizza

Ingredients:

- 1 pizza dough
- 1/2 cup taco sauce
- 2 cups shredded cheddar cheese
- 1 cup cooked ground beef or chicken, seasoned with taco seasoning
- 1/4 cup red onion, chopped
- 1/4 cup diced tomatoes
- 1/4 cup sliced black olives
- Fresh cilantro, for garnish
- Sour cream, for topping

Instructions:

1. Preheat oven to 475°F (245°C).
2. Roll out the pizza dough and place it on a pizza stone or baking sheet.
3. Spread taco sauce over the dough.
4. Top with shredded cheddar cheese, cooked ground beef or chicken, red onion, tomatoes, and black olives.
5. Bake for 10-12 minutes until the crust is golden and the cheese is melted.
6. Garnish with fresh cilantro and serve with a dollop of sour cream.

Fajita Chicken Pizza

Ingredients:

- 1 pizza dough
- 1/2 cup salsa
- 2 cups shredded mozzarella cheese
- 1 cup cooked chicken, sliced
- 1/4 cup bell peppers, sliced
- 1/4 cup red onion, sliced
- 1/4 cup corn kernels (optional)
- Fresh cilantro, for garnish
- Lime wedges, for serving

Instructions:

1. Preheat oven to 475°F (245°C).
2. Roll out the pizza dough and transfer to a pizza stone or baking sheet.
3. Spread salsa over the dough.
4. Top with shredded mozzarella cheese, sliced chicken, bell peppers, red onion, and corn (if using).
5. Bake for 10-12 minutes until the crust is golden and the cheese is melted.
6. Garnish with fresh cilantro and serve with lime wedges.

Prosciutto and Arugula Pizza

Ingredients:

- 1 pizza dough
- 1/2 cup pizza sauce
- 2 cups shredded mozzarella cheese
- 4-6 slices prosciutto
- Fresh arugula
- Olive oil, for drizzling
- Balsamic glaze, for drizzling

Instructions:

1. Preheat oven to 475°F (245°C).
2. Roll out the pizza dough and place it on a pizza stone or baking sheet.
3. Spread pizza sauce over the dough.
4. Sprinkle with shredded mozzarella cheese.
5. Bake for 10-12 minutes until the crust is golden and the cheese is melted.
6. After baking, top with prosciutto slices and fresh arugula.
7. Drizzle with olive oil and balsamic glaze, slice, and serve.

Smoked Salmon Pizza

Ingredients:

- 1 pizza dough
- 1/2 cup cream cheese, softened
- 1/4 cup sour cream
- 1/2 cup shredded mozzarella cheese
- 4-6 slices smoked salmon
- Red onion, thinly sliced
- Fresh dill, for garnish
- Lemon wedges, for serving

Instructions:

1. Preheat oven to 475°F (245°C).
2. Roll out the pizza dough and transfer to a pizza stone or baking sheet.
3. Mix cream cheese and sour cream together, then spread evenly over the dough.
4. Sprinkle shredded mozzarella cheese on top.
5. Bake for 10-12 minutes until the crust is golden and the cheese is melted.
6. After baking, top with smoked salmon, red onion slices, and fresh dill.
7. Serve with lemon wedges.

Eggplant Parmesan Pizza

Ingredients:

- 1 pizza dough
- 1/2 cup marinara sauce
- 2 cups shredded mozzarella cheese
- 1/2 cup grated Parmesan cheese
- 1 small eggplant, thinly sliced and roasted
- Fresh basil leaves, for garnish

Instructions:

1. Preheat oven to 475°F (245°C).
2. Roll out the pizza dough and place it on a pizza stone or baking sheet.
3. Spread marinara sauce over the dough.
4. Sprinkle with shredded mozzarella and grated Parmesan cheeses.
5. Top with roasted eggplant slices.
6. Bake for 10-12 minutes until the crust is golden and the cheese is melted.
7. Garnish with fresh basil leaves and serve.

BBQ Beef Pizza

Ingredients:

- 1 pizza dough
- 1/2 cup BBQ sauce
- 2 cups shredded mozzarella cheese
- 1 cup cooked beef, shredded
- 1/4 cup red onion, thinly sliced
- Fresh cilantro, for garnish

Instructions:

1. Preheat oven to 475°F (245°C).
2. Roll out the pizza dough and transfer to a pizza stone or baking sheet.
3. Spread BBQ sauce over the dough.
4. Sprinkle with shredded mozzarella cheese.
5. Top with shredded beef and red onion slices.
6. Bake for 10-12 minutes until the crust is golden and the cheese is melted.
7. Garnish with fresh cilantro and slice.

Bacon and Onion Pizza

Ingredients:

- 1 pizza dough
- 1/2 cup pizza sauce
- 2 cups shredded mozzarella cheese
- 6 slices cooked bacon, crumbled
- 1/4 cup red onion, thinly sliced
- Olive oil, for drizzling

Instructions:

1. Preheat oven to 475°F (245°C).
2. Roll out the pizza dough and place it on a pizza stone or baking sheet.
3. Spread pizza sauce over the dough.
4. Sprinkle with shredded mozzarella cheese.
5. Top with crumbled bacon and red onion slices.
6. Bake for 10-12 minutes until the crust is golden and the cheese is melted.
7. Drizzle with olive oil and serve.

Roasted Garlic and Rosemary Pizza

Ingredients:

- 1 pizza dough
- 1/2 cup olive oil
- 3-4 cloves roasted garlic, mashed
- 2 cups shredded mozzarella cheese
- Fresh rosemary, finely chopped
- Salt and pepper, to taste

Instructions:

1. Preheat oven to 475°F (245°C).
2. Roll out the pizza dough and transfer to a pizza stone or baking sheet.
3. Mix olive oil and roasted garlic, then spread over the dough.
4. Sprinkle with shredded mozzarella cheese and fresh rosemary.
5. Season with salt and pepper.
6. Bake for 10-12 minutes until the crust is golden and the cheese is melted.
7. Slice and serve.

Veggie Pesto Pizza

Ingredients:

- 1 pizza dough
- 1/2 cup pesto sauce
- 2 cups shredded mozzarella cheese
- 1/4 cup bell peppers, sliced
- 1/4 cup red onion, thinly sliced
- 1/4 cup zucchini, thinly sliced
- Fresh basil leaves, for garnish

Instructions:

1. Preheat oven to 475°F (245°C).
2. Roll out the pizza dough and place it on a pizza stone or baking sheet.
3. Spread pesto sauce over the dough.
4. Sprinkle with shredded mozzarella cheese.
5. Top with bell peppers, red onion, and zucchini slices.
6. Bake for 10-12 minutes until the crust is golden and the cheese is melted.
7. Garnish with fresh basil leaves and slice.

Peppadew and Goat Cheese Pizza

Ingredients:

- 1 pizza dough
- 1/2 cup pizza sauce
- 2 cups shredded mozzarella cheese
- 1/4 cup peppadew peppers, sliced
- 1/4 cup goat cheese, crumbled
- Fresh arugula, for garnish

Instructions:

1. Preheat oven to 475°F (245°C).
2. Roll out the pizza dough and place it on a pizza stone or baking sheet.
3. Spread pizza sauce over the dough.
4. Sprinkle with shredded mozzarella cheese.
5. Top with peppadew peppers and crumbled goat cheese.
6. Bake for 10-12 minutes until the crust is golden and the cheese is melted.
7. Garnish with fresh arugula and serve.

Breakfast Pizza

Ingredients:

- 1 pizza dough
- 1/2 cup cream cheese, softened
- 1/4 cup shredded mozzarella cheese
- 4-6 scrambled eggs
- 2-3 slices cooked bacon, crumbled
- 1/4 cup sausage, cooked and crumbled
- Fresh parsley, for garnish

Instructions:

1. Preheat oven to 475°F (245°C).
2. Roll out the pizza dough and transfer to a pizza stone or baking sheet.
3. Spread cream cheese over the dough, then sprinkle with shredded mozzarella cheese.
4. Top with scrambled eggs, crumbled bacon, and sausage.
5. Bake for 10-12 minutes until the crust is golden and the cheese is melted.
6. Garnish with fresh parsley and serve.

Zaa'tar Pizza

Ingredients:

- 1 pizza dough
- 1/4 cup olive oil
- 2 tbsp za'atar spice mix
- 2 cups shredded mozzarella cheese
- Fresh lemon juice
- Fresh parsley, for garnish

Instructions:

1. Preheat oven to 475°F (245°C).
2. Roll out the pizza dough and place it on a pizza stone or baking sheet.
3. Mix olive oil and za'atar, then brush the mixture over the dough.
4. Sprinkle with shredded mozzarella cheese.
5. Bake for 10-12 minutes until the crust is golden and the cheese is melted.
6. Drizzle with fresh lemon juice and garnish with fresh parsley before serving.

Ranch Chicken Pizza

Ingredients:

- 1 pizza dough
- 1/2 cup ranch dressing
- 2 cups shredded mozzarella cheese
- 1 cup cooked chicken, shredded
- 1/4 cup red onion, thinly sliced
- 1/4 cup bacon bits
- Fresh parsley, for garnish

Instructions:

1. Preheat oven to 475°F (245°C).
2. Roll out the pizza dough and place it on a pizza stone or baking sheet.
3. Spread ranch dressing over the dough.
4. Top with shredded mozzarella cheese, shredded chicken, red onion, and bacon bits.
5. Bake for 10-12 minutes until the crust is golden and the cheese is melted.
6. Garnish with fresh parsley and serve.

Cheeseburger Pizza

Ingredients:

- 1 pizza dough
- 1/2 cup ketchup
- 1/4 cup mustard
- 2 cups shredded mozzarella cheese
- 1 cup cooked ground beef, seasoned with salt and pepper
- 1/4 cup red onion, chopped
- 1/4 cup pickles, sliced
- Lettuce, for garnish

Instructions:

1. Preheat oven to 475°F (245°C).
2. Roll out the pizza dough and transfer to a pizza stone or baking sheet.
3. Mix ketchup and mustard, then spread over the dough.
4. Sprinkle with shredded mozzarella cheese and top with cooked ground beef, red onion, and pickles.
5. Bake for 10-12 minutes until the crust is golden and the cheese is melted.
6. Garnish with fresh lettuce before serving.

Sweet Potato and Bacon Pizza

Ingredients:

- 1 pizza dough
- 1/2 cup olive oil
- 1 medium sweet potato, thinly sliced
- 2 cups shredded mozzarella cheese
- 4 slices cooked bacon, crumbled
- Fresh rosemary, for garnish

Instructions:

1. Preheat oven to 475°F (245°C).
2. Roll out the pizza dough and transfer to a pizza stone or baking sheet.
3. Brush olive oil over the dough and top with shredded mozzarella cheese.
4. Arrange thinly sliced sweet potato evenly on the pizza.
5. Sprinkle crumbled bacon over the top.
6. Bake for 10-12 minutes until the crust is golden and the cheese is melted.
7. Garnish with fresh rosemary and serve.

Buffalo Cauliflower Pizza

Ingredients:

- 1 pizza dough
- 1/2 cup buffalo sauce
- 2 cups shredded mozzarella cheese
- 2 cups cauliflower florets, roasted
- 1/4 cup blue cheese, crumbled
- Fresh parsley, for garnish

Instructions:

1. Preheat oven to 475°F (245°C).
2. Roll out the pizza dough and place it on a pizza stone or baking sheet.
3. Spread buffalo sauce over the dough and sprinkle with shredded mozzarella cheese.
4. Top with roasted cauliflower and crumbled blue cheese.
5. Bake for 10-12 minutes until the crust is golden and the cheese is melted.
6. Garnish with fresh parsley and serve.

Greek Pizza

Ingredients:

- 1 pizza dough
- 1/2 cup tzatziki sauce
- 2 cups shredded mozzarella cheese
- 1/4 cup red onion, thinly sliced
- 1/4 cup Kalamata olives, sliced
- 1/4 cup feta cheese, crumbled
- Fresh oregano, for garnish

Instructions:

1. Preheat oven to 475°F (245°C).
2. Roll out the pizza dough and transfer to a pizza stone or baking sheet.
3. Spread tzatziki sauce over the dough.
4. Sprinkle with shredded mozzarella cheese and top with red onion, Kalamata olives, and crumbled feta cheese.
5. Bake for 10-12 minutes until the crust is golden and the cheese is melted.
6. Garnish with fresh oregano before serving.

Fig and Prosciutto Pizza

Ingredients:

- 1 pizza dough
- 1/2 cup olive oil
- 2 cups shredded mozzarella cheese
- 4-6 fresh figs, sliced
- 4 slices prosciutto
- Fresh arugula, for garnish
- Balsamic glaze, for drizzling

Instructions:

1. Preheat oven to 475°F (245°C).
2. Roll out the pizza dough and transfer to a pizza stone or baking sheet.
3. Brush olive oil over the dough and top with shredded mozzarella cheese.
4. Arrange sliced figs evenly over the pizza.
5. Bake for 10-12 minutes until the crust is golden and the cheese is melted.
6. After baking, top with prosciutto and fresh arugula.
7. Drizzle with balsamic glaze before serving.

Caramelized Onion and Blue Cheese Pizza

Ingredients:

- 1 pizza dough
- 1/2 cup olive oil
- 2 large onions, caramelized
- 2 cups shredded mozzarella cheese
- 1/4 cup blue cheese, crumbled
- Fresh thyme, for garnish

Instructions:

1. Preheat oven to 475°F (245°C).
2. Roll out the pizza dough and transfer to a pizza stone or baking sheet.
3. Brush olive oil over the dough and top with shredded mozzarella cheese.
4. Spread caramelized onions evenly over the pizza.
5. Sprinkle crumbled blue cheese over the top.
6. Bake for 10-12 minutes until the crust is golden and the cheese is melted.
7. Garnish with fresh thyme before serving.

Spicy Sausage Pizza

Ingredients:

- 1 pizza dough
- 1/2 cup marinara sauce
- 2 cups shredded mozzarella cheese
- 1 cup spicy Italian sausage, cooked and crumbled
- 1/4 cup red onion, thinly sliced
- 1/4 tsp red pepper flakes (optional)
- Fresh basil leaves, for garnish

Instructions:

1. Preheat oven to 475°F (245°C).
2. Roll out the pizza dough and place it on a pizza stone or baking sheet.
3. Spread marinara sauce over the dough.
4. Sprinkle with shredded mozzarella cheese and top with cooked sausage, red onion, and red pepper flakes.
5. Bake for 10-12 minutes until the crust is golden and the cheese is melted.
6. Garnish with fresh basil before serving.

Pear and Gorgonzola Pizza

Ingredients:

- 1 pizza dough
- 1/2 cup olive oil
- 2 cups shredded mozzarella cheese
- 1 pear, thinly sliced
- 1/4 cup crumbled Gorgonzola cheese
- 1/4 cup walnuts, chopped
- Fresh arugula, for garnish
- Honey, for drizzling

Instructions:

1. Preheat oven to 475°F (245°C).
2. Roll out the pizza dough and transfer to a pizza stone or baking sheet.
3. Brush olive oil over the dough and top with shredded mozzarella cheese.
4. Arrange pear slices evenly on the pizza and sprinkle with crumbled Gorgonzola cheese.
5. Add chopped walnuts over the top.
6. Bake for 10-12 minutes until the crust is golden and the cheese is melted.
7. After baking, garnish with fresh arugula and drizzle with honey before serving.

Chicken Caesar Pizza

Ingredients:

- 1 pizza dough
- 1/2 cup Caesar dressing
- 2 cups shredded mozzarella cheese
- 1 cup cooked chicken breast, shredded
- 1/4 cup Parmesan cheese, grated
- 1/4 cup romaine lettuce, chopped
- Fresh parsley, for garnish

Instructions:

1. Preheat oven to 475°F (245°C).
2. Roll out the pizza dough and transfer to a pizza stone or baking sheet.
3. Spread Caesar dressing over the dough.
4. Sprinkle with shredded mozzarella cheese and top with shredded chicken.
5. Bake for 10-12 minutes until the crust is golden and the cheese is melted.
6. After baking, sprinkle with grated Parmesan cheese and top with chopped romaine lettuce and fresh parsley before serving.

Hot Honey and Pepperoni Pizza

Ingredients:

- 1 pizza dough
- 1/2 cup marinara sauce
- 2 cups shredded mozzarella cheese
- 20-25 slices of pepperoni
- 2 tbsp hot honey
- Fresh basil, for garnish

Instructions:

1. Preheat oven to 475°F (245°C).
2. Roll out the pizza dough and transfer to a pizza stone or baking sheet.
3. Spread marinara sauce over the dough.
4. Sprinkle with shredded mozzarella cheese and arrange pepperoni slices evenly on top.
5. Bake for 10-12 minutes until the crust is golden and the cheese is melted.
6. Drizzle with hot honey and garnish with fresh basil before serving.

Vegan Margherita Pizza

Ingredients:

- 1 pizza dough
- 1/2 cup marinara sauce
- 2 cups vegan mozzarella cheese
- 2 tomatoes, thinly sliced
- Fresh basil leaves
- Olive oil, for drizzling

Instructions:

1. Preheat oven to 475°F (245°C).
2. Roll out the pizza dough and transfer to a pizza stone or baking sheet.
3. Spread marinara sauce over the dough.
4. Top with vegan mozzarella cheese and arrange tomato slices evenly on top.
5. Bake for 10-12 minutes until the crust is golden and the cheese is melted.
6. After baking, garnish with fresh basil leaves and drizzle with olive oil before serving.

Ricotta and Lemon Zest Pizza

Ingredients:

- 1 pizza dough
- 1/2 cup ricotta cheese
- 2 cups shredded mozzarella cheese
- 1 lemon, zested
- Fresh thyme leaves
- Olive oil, for drizzling

Instructions:

1. Preheat oven to 475°F (245°C).
2. Roll out the pizza dough and transfer to a pizza stone or baking sheet.
3. Spread ricotta cheese over the dough and top with shredded mozzarella cheese.
4. Sprinkle lemon zest over the top and add fresh thyme leaves.
5. Bake for 10-12 minutes until the crust is golden and the cheese is melted.
6. Drizzle with olive oil before serving.

Lobster and Lemon Pizza

Ingredients:

- 1 pizza dough
- 1/2 cup olive oil
- 2 cups shredded mozzarella cheese
- 1 cup cooked lobster meat, chopped
- 1 lemon, thinly sliced
- 2 tbsp fresh parsley, chopped
- Fresh arugula, for garnish

Instructions:

1. Preheat oven to 475°F (245°C).
2. Roll out the pizza dough and transfer to a pizza stone or baking sheet.
3. Brush olive oil over the dough and top with shredded mozzarella cheese.
4. Arrange lemon slices and chopped lobster meat evenly over the pizza.
5. Bake for 10-12 minutes until the crust is golden and the cheese is melted.
6. After baking, garnish with fresh parsley and arugula before serving.

Chili and Cheese Pizza

Ingredients:

- 1 pizza dough
- 1/2 cup chili (cooked and thickened)
- 2 cups shredded cheddar cheese
- 1/4 cup red onion, thinly sliced
- 1/4 cup jalapeños, sliced
- 1/4 cup sour cream, for drizzling
- Fresh cilantro, for garnish

Instructions:

1. Preheat oven to 475°F (245°C).
2. Roll out the pizza dough and transfer to a pizza stone or baking sheet.
3. Spread the cooked chili over the dough.
4. Sprinkle with shredded cheddar cheese, and top with red onion slices and jalapeños.
5. Bake for 10-12 minutes until the crust is golden and the cheese is melted.
6. After baking, drizzle with sour cream and garnish with fresh cilantro before serving.

Puttanesca Pizza

Ingredients:

- 1 pizza dough
- 1/2 cup marinara sauce
- 2 cups shredded mozzarella cheese
- 1/4 cup black olives, sliced
- 1/4 cup capers
- 1/4 cup red onion, thinly sliced
- 1/2 tsp red pepper flakes (optional)
- Fresh basil, for garnish

Instructions:

1. Preheat oven to 475°F (245°C).
2. Roll out the pizza dough and transfer to a pizza stone or baking sheet.
3. Spread marinara sauce over the dough and sprinkle with shredded mozzarella cheese.
4. Top with black olives, capers, and red onion slices. Add red pepper flakes for extra heat if desired.
5. Bake for 10-12 minutes until the crust is golden and the cheese is melted.
6. Garnish with fresh basil before serving.

Roasted Beet and Goat Cheese Pizza

Ingredients:

- 1 pizza dough
- 1/2 cup olive oil
- 2 cups shredded mozzarella cheese
- 1 medium roasted beet, peeled and sliced
- 1/4 cup crumbled goat cheese
- 1 tbsp fresh thyme leaves
- Arugula, for garnish
- Balsamic glaze, for drizzling

Instructions:

1. Preheat oven to 475°F (245°C).
2. Roll out the pizza dough and transfer to a pizza stone or baking sheet.
3. Brush olive oil over the dough and sprinkle with shredded mozzarella cheese.
4. Arrange roasted beet slices evenly on the pizza and sprinkle with crumbled goat cheese.
5. Bake for 10-12 minutes until the crust is golden and the cheese is melted.
6. After baking, sprinkle with fresh thyme, garnish with arugula, and drizzle with balsamic glaze before serving.

Cilantro Lime Chicken Pizza

Ingredients:

- 1 pizza dough
- 1/2 cup salsa or marinara sauce
- 2 cups shredded mozzarella cheese
- 1 cup cooked chicken breast, shredded
- 1/4 cup red onion, thinly sliced
- 1 tbsp lime juice
- Fresh cilantro, for garnish

Instructions:

1. Preheat oven to 475°F (245°C).
2. Roll out the pizza dough and transfer to a pizza stone or baking sheet.
3. Spread salsa or marinara sauce over the dough and sprinkle with shredded mozzarella cheese.
4. Top with shredded chicken and red onion slices.
5. Bake for 10-12 minutes until the crust is golden and the cheese is melted.
6. After baking, drizzle with lime juice and garnish with fresh cilantro before serving.

Balsamic Glazed Chicken Pizza

Ingredients:

- 1 pizza dough
- 1/2 cup balsamic glaze
- 2 cups shredded mozzarella cheese
- 1 cup cooked chicken breast, sliced
- 1/4 cup red onion, thinly sliced
- Fresh spinach, for garnish

Instructions:

1. Preheat oven to 475°F (245°C).
2. Roll out the pizza dough and transfer to a pizza stone or baking sheet.
3. Drizzle balsamic glaze over the dough and sprinkle with shredded mozzarella cheese.

4. Top with sliced chicken breast and red onion slices.
5. Bake for 10-12 minutes until the crust is golden and the cheese is melted.
6. After baking, garnish with fresh spinach before serving.